MW01122982

The call of the Disciples

ILLUSTRATIONS BY CHANTAL MULLER VAN DEN BERGHE
TEXT BY BERNARD HUBLER

3

Distributed in the United Kingdom and Ireland by:
MATTHEW JAMES PUBLISHING Ltd
19 Wellington Close
Chelmsford, Essex CM1 2EE
Tel: 01245 347 710
Fax: 01245 347 713

Distributed in Canada by:
NOVALIS
49 Front St. E, 2nd Floor
Toronto, ON M5E 1B3
Tel: 1-800-387-7164
Fax (416) 363-9409

Translation by Oliver Todd
Created by Jacques Rey

© Éditions du Signe 1998
Strasbourg - France
All rights reserved
Printed in Italy by Albagraf - Pomezia (Roma)
ISBN 1-898366-50-0

Quotations from the gospels are from Mark 1:16:18, Matthew 9:9 and John 1:43-46.

The gospels tell us how Jesus
gathered a team of people around him.
He called some of them himself;
others were brought by their friends.
Jesus asked them to leave everything behind
and follow him on a great adventure.
As they got to know him,
he prepared them to become
the first leaders of the Christian communities.

"Jesus saw Simon and his brother Andrew."

Jesus is walking along the edge of Lake Galilee.
Two brothers, Simon and Andrew,
are busy fishing.
Jesus watches them casting their nets.
It's nice to see a fisherman casting his net.

*It's worth taking the trouble
to stop and watch someone working.*

"He said to them: Come with me"

Jesus says to himself: I need a team,
and there are two people who could help me
to travel around the villages
proclaiming the Good News.
He shouts to them: "Hey you two! Come with me!"

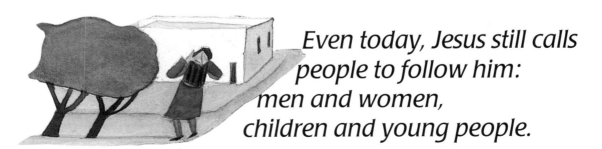

Even today, Jesus still calls
people to follow him:
men and women,
children and young people.

"*I will make you fishers of men and women*"

When they came to Jesus, he said to them:
"Come on! I need you.
I'll make you fishers of men and women."
  Andrew and Simon don't understand
  what this will really mean.
  But they trust him.
  They leave their nets and follow him.

*Jesus is calling us to proclaim his Good News
and to get together with those who believe it.*

"Jesus saw a man named Matthew."

One day, Jesus leaves Capernaum,
a little village by the lakeside.

He sees a man sitting at his desk,
collecting taxes.
He does not look very happy.
In those days people did not like tax collectors.

Let's go beyond what people look like,
and let's see what they're really like inside.

"*Jesus said to him: Follow me.*"

The tax collector was called Matthew.
Jesus stops in front of him,
looks at him and simply says:
"Matthew, follow me."
Matthew gets up right away
and he follows Jesus.

We don't just follow anyone.
We need to trust someone
that we are following.

"*Jesus meets Philip.*"

This took place in Galilee
a few days later.
Jesus meets Philip
and he calls him: "Follow me."
Philip was from Bethsaida,
a fishing village at the north of the lake.

*To follow a person we sometimes have to leave
our area, our town and all the things we are used to*

"Philip meets Nathaniel."

Jesus calls some men to follow him.
They then begin to call other people.
Philip introduces Nathaniel to Jesus
to strengthen the team.

*You can't do that much
on your own.
But as part of a team
you can do more.*

"We have found the one whom the prophets talk about."

Philip is very keen.
He tells Nathaniel:
"We have found the man
that Moses and the prophets talk about.
He is Jesus, Joseph's son, from Nazareth."
Moses and the prophets talked about
a very special man who was going to come.

When you get some good news,
you don't keep it to yourself.
You rush out to tell other people!

"Can anything good come from Nazareth?"

Nathaniel wasn't very convinced.
He wondered whether such a great
and powerful man could come
from such a small village as Nazareth,
a man who was going to bring
happiness to people
who were so unhappy.

*Sometimes we don't realise
that we are surrounded by really
wonderful people.*

"Come, and you'll see!"

Philip insists: "Come, and you'll see!"
It's true.
He didn't have to say "yes" right away
like the others who left everything to follow Jesus.
Nathaniel obviously needed more time.
But finally he too joined the team.

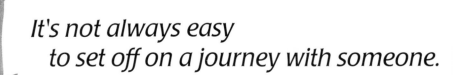

*It's not always easy
to set off on a journey with someone.*

This is how Jesus gradually gathered his team around him.
We too are invited to join the team:
to love one another,
to get to know Jesus better,
to live like he asks us,
to make him known to others.
It's as a team, a community,
that we make up the Church of Jesus.
Today Jesus speaks once more to each of us,
and he says:
"Come and follow me!"

"Jesus saw Simon and his brother Andrew."

6

10

"He said to them: Come with me"

8

"I will make you fishers of men and women"

"Jesus saw a man named Matthew."

12

14

"Jesus said to him: Follow me."

"Jesus meets Philip."

"Philip meets Nathaniel."

"We have found the one whom the prophets talk about."

"Come, and you'll see!"

"Can anything good come from Nazareth?"

In the same
collection:

Bartimaeus
Zacchaeus
The Good Samaritan
The Paralysed Man
The Calming of the Storm
The Prodigal Son
Shared Bread
The Amazing Catch
The Forgiven Sinner
The Sower
The Disciples from Emmaus